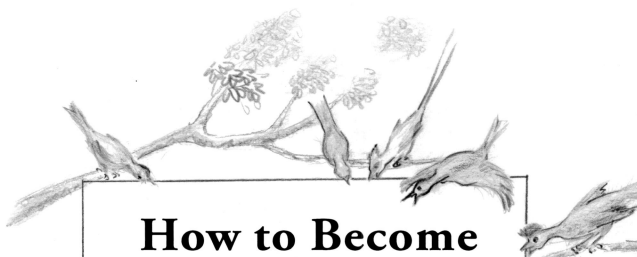

How to Become
PRESIDENT

By Erika Nielsen

D1439321

ISBN: 978-1-7345059-2-4

FOREWORD

How to Become President is primarily intended to educate children about the basics of the election process by introducing relevant vocabulary and concepts in a light, humorous and engaging way. It is not a dry recitation of rules and procedures; it provides a glimpse of the passions and sentiments surrounding elections without delving into political differences.

The book is written within the paradigm of fables, a well-established educational model that has been used by our ancestors from around the world for thousands of years to teach children. Through the use of characters, the book demonstrates which personal qualities and skills, such as resilience, self-control and a balanced, well-reasoned debating style, can lead to success and what personal weaknesses can lead to failure.

We all hope that our future generations will be wise and just. We all do our best to provide them with the knowledge they need to achieve that goal.

To all of our future voters
and future politicians:
We love you and we wish you
happiness and success!

Hi! My name is Lorenzo the Lion. I am strong and brave.

I will work hard to make the jungle a safe and friendly place, where animals help each other and where we all will have a brighter future.

Please, elect me as your President!

MEET THE CANDIDATES

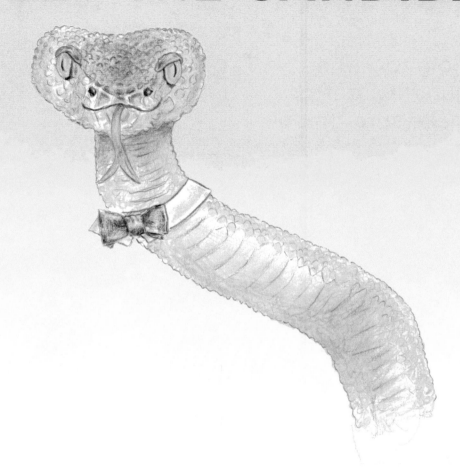

Hi! My name is Shasu the Snake. I am smart and nimble. I can climb the highest trees. I talk to many animals: ones who live on the ground, ones who live on the highest branches and to all the rest in between. I listen to all of you and I can make all of your dreams come true!

Vote for me! I will be the best president ever!

Lorenzo:

"We have to join together to make the jungle a better place! I will make sure that all of the animals can drink water in peace. Birds and gazelles will drink from the river and not worry about anyone sneaking up on them.

We can build a team of animals to fight forest fires to keep our homes safe.

Together, we can achieve great things!"

5

Shasu:

"So, animals, tell me what it is you want."

"We want to make the rules, because we know what to do!" screamed the monkeys. "We are very smart!"

"I am tall! I don't need rules. I can see everything for myself" said the giraffe.

"I want to keep my nest safe," said a bird.

"But I am hungry" said a crocodile.

"Oh, no!" said Shasu. "I can't make all you happy at the same time!"

"Oh, well..." said the animals. "That's too bad..."

Shasu decided to go out and make some friends.

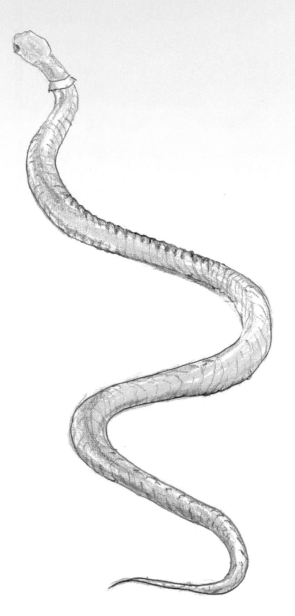

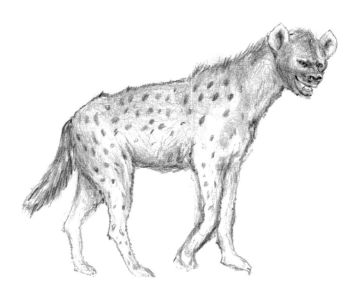

MEESHA THE HYENA

KEESHA THE JACKAL

MAKING FRIENDS

GREESHA THE VULTURE

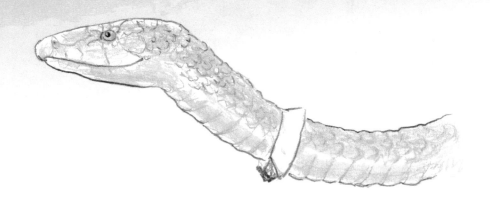

First, Shasu asked Meesha, the hyena:

"Hey, Meesha, my buddy, do you want to be in charge of education?"

"What's that?"

"School. Do you want to be the most important guy in school?"

"Yep." Ha, Ha Haaa...!

"Keesha, You are so smart! How would you like to be in charge of the Treasury?"

"Oh, yes! That would be marvelous!

I love treasure!"

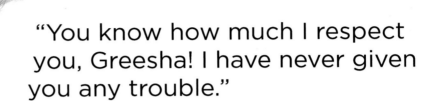

"You know how much I respect you, Greesha! I have never given you any trouble."

"You wouldn't dare. I have a sharp beak."

"How would you like to be Secretary of Defense?"

"And if there is a war?"

"You will be the first to know about it."

"No use. I will never be confirmed. No one loves me. I smell bad."

"Of course you will be confirmed. You look like the most distinguished, handsome bird."

"You think so?"

"Highly respectable! Just don't let them get close enough to smell you."

16

"I will be proud to serve our common goal!" said Greesha, puffing out his chest.

"All right! We'll make a great team," said Shasu.

"The only problem is, everyone really likes Lorenzo. He is very popular," noted Keesha.

"We'll have to make him less popular, "said Shasu.

"How?" asked his friends.

"We have to run a **negative campaign.**"

"What's that?"

"We have to say bad things about Lorenzo," whispered Shasu.

"But we don't know any bad things about Lorenzo."

"Be quiet... We'll have to come up with something. Otherwise all the animals will vote for him!"

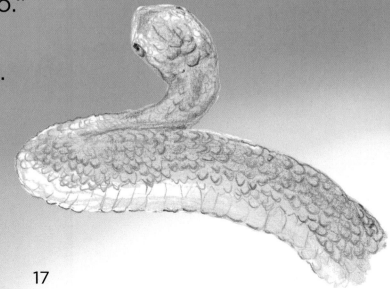

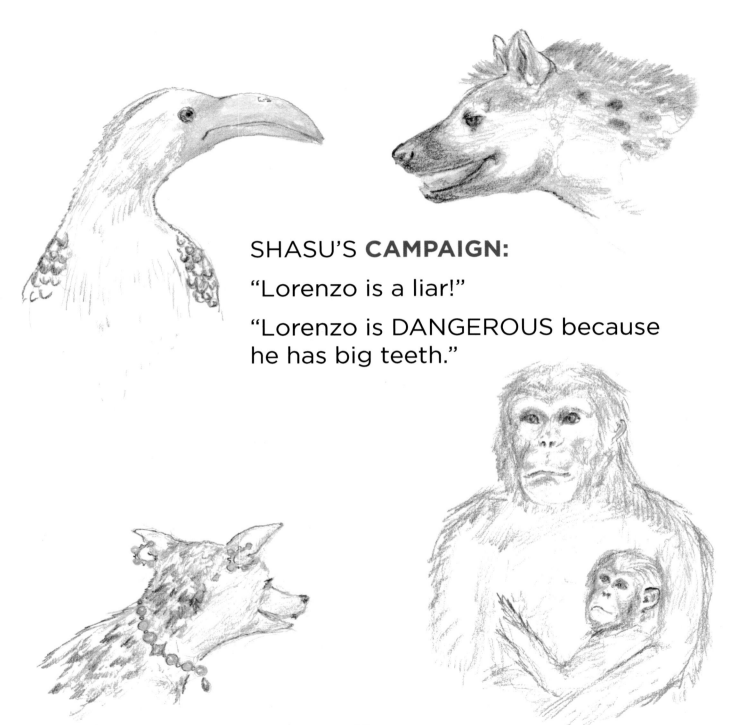

SHASU'S **CAMPAIGN:**

"Lorenzo is a liar!"

"Lorenzo is DANGEROUS because he has big teeth."

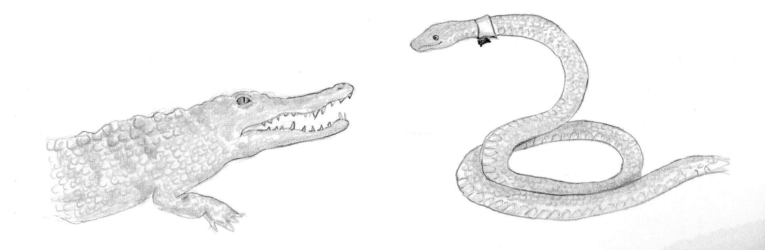

"Lorenzo is not even from the jungle. He needs to go back to the grassland and eat grass!"

LORENZO'S CAMPAIGN:

Lorenzo had a very bad day. He went to see his advisor, Benjamin the Gorilla.

"I should never have run for president! How can I hunt now? Everywhere I go, there is great noise in front of me: squawking, squealing, shouting and whistling! When I stop, I see no one; I only hear whispers in the grass and in the trees…"

Benjamin rubbed his chin. "What are they whispering?" he asked.

"I don't think they like me any more…"

"Whispers change, like the wind, said Benjamin. You have to win the **debate!**"

21

"I will roar and everyone will know how great I am! Listen to this: GRRRAAAAH!"

"They are already afraid of you. You need to be nice and smile, but don't show your teeth!"

"That will be hard. I feel angry. I heard them call me names..."

"When you will win, they will call you Mr. President!"

PRESIDENTIAL DEBATE

"Lorenzo, are you a lion?" asked Shasu.

"Yes."

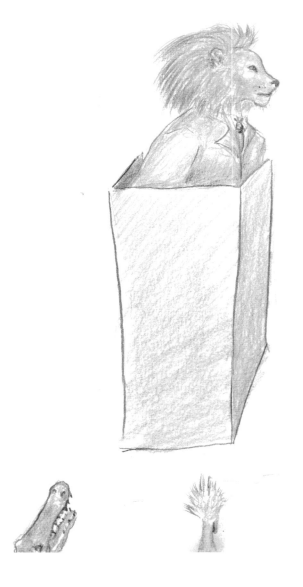

"Lion! Li....on. Lie! Lorenzo is a liar! Liar! Liar!"

"That doesn't make sense. If you want to call me a liar, you have to prove that I have lied. Can you prove that?"

"No, but I can prove you are DANGEROUS! Open your mouth and let everyone see what big teeth you have!"

"Yes, I have big teeth. All lions have big teeth when they grow up. You have no paws, but I don't hold it against you, because you were born that way. Snakes have no paws and that's OK; everyone is different. For example, both of us have no wings and we can't fly. Does that make us bad candidates?"

"No, of course not. But I know something else about you. You don't know how to share, because you are a lion. Have you all heard what a 'lion's share' is?"

"We know! We know!" screamed Keesha and Meesha. "That's when the lion takes most of the food. He eats the best parts and leaves us only scraps. That's not fair!"

"I have heard that saying about Lions, but I am not like that", said Lorenzo. "I always share the food fairly. So, Shasu, since you know so much about sharing, why don't you tell us how you will share if you become President."

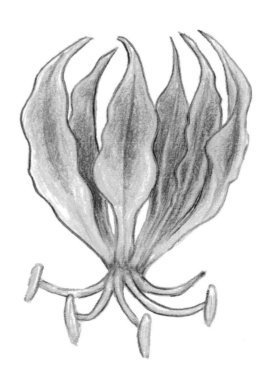

"I will put Greesha in charge of the army, Keesha in charge of the Treasury and Meesha in charge of Education. I will make all of them very important!" proudly said Shasu.

"So, you know how to share with your friends. That's nice, but if you become president, you will be EVERYONE'S president. If I become president, I will make sure that EVERYONE will get a fair share."

On **voting** day, all animals went to the polls. Each animal got a **secret ballot.** Everyone marked the name of one candidate on the ballot, without telling anyone who's name they chose.

They all waited their turn to cast their ballots into the box.

After that, all the ballots were counted.

Lorenzo got more votes than Shasu. Shasu felt sad, but he didn't show it.

He **conceded the election** to Lorenzo.

He said: "You won, Lorenzo. Congratulations!"

INAUGURATION

Lorenzo stood at the podium in front of all the voters and said: "I solemnly swear that I will serve all the animals of the jungle. I will work to protect and defend fairness and justice for all animals."

CELEBRATION

After that everyone wanted to celebrate. The animals danced at the beautiful **inauguration ball.** They were very happy and had a great time.

THE END

ACKNOWLEDGEMENTS

I would like to thank my dear husband, who has been very kind and supportive in every way. I thank my son, who had the original idea for this book that would have never been written without him.

I have learned a lot, being a mother of a high school debate team member, and I am grateful to my son for giving me that amazing experience.

My daughter's beautiful artwork was the source of my inspiration for illustrating this book. When I had a lot of doubt about the quality of my own artwork, she gave me some very wise advice: "Don't let the perfect be the enemy of the good." Without that advice, the work on this book may never have been completed.

I thank my dear friend, Annemarie, who is an excellent artist, writer and illustrator and I wish her success in her work, as well as my friend Karen, who's wisdom and kindness inspire me to become a better person. I thank my graphic designer, Annette, for her brilliant work and excellent advice. I thank my friends and family for their support and encouragement. I really appreciate your feedback on this book.

Erika Nielsen

Made in the USA
Middletown, DE
08 August 2023

36050580R00024